KU-610-172

Sponsored by

Building Design Partnership was formed in 1961 as an integrated practice of architects and engineers. Our multidisciplinary approach to urbanism brings together town planners, landscape designers, urban designers and others. Add to this our experience of developing world-class retail facilities, offices leisure, transport interchanges and housing, and BDP can create schemes that work for the community 24 hours a day. Today, BDP has six offices in the UK and Ireland, associations in France, Spain and Germany under the collective name of BDP International SC, and projects world-wide.

David Lock Associates is one of the UK's leading town planning and urban design consultancies. Established in 1988, we now employ over 50 professional staff in our office in Milton Keynes. The experience of our consultants spans planning and urban design and the related disciplines of architecture, development, landscape and graphic design. We have extensive experience gained working for a variety of agencies and organisations both in the UK and oversees. This strong multidisciplinary base enables us to offer a complete range of planning and urban design services, from inception through to implementation on the ground.

Roger Evans Associates are engaged in research, design and the delivery of high quality, sustainable urban environments. Architects, planners and landscape architects, they have actively contributed to developing the current urban design agenda drawing on their wide experience in preparing quarter frameworks and masterplans for city centres and town extensions in the UK and abroad.

Sheppard Robson are an integrated practice of award winning planners, urban designers and architects. The scope of work includes feasibility studies, strategic planning, urban regeneration, development planning, urban design, master planning, new settlement planning and tourism development. Through its joint venture practice Sheppard Robson Corgan there are associated offices across the USA.

Terence O'Rourke plc Terence O'Rourke plc is an award winning practice dedicated to creating successful environments. Formed in 1985, we now have a team of more than eighty professional staff and alongside town planning, urban design and master planning, the practice also specialises in environmental consultancy, landscape architecture, architecture and graphic design. The art of making successful places in which to live, work and relax is central to good urban design, and our approach is designed to add lasting value for the benefit of both the investor and the community as a whole.

WS Atkins is one of the world's leading providers of professional, technologically-based consultancy and support services. Atkins operates from 175 offices around the world and employs over 15,000 permanent staff. The company provides services to government departments and national agencies, local authorities, industry and the private sector both at home and worldwide. The planning, landscape and urban design consultancy provides services in urban planning and conservation, traffic management, landscape and urban design and in public consultation, with offices in Epsom, London, Birmingham, Manchester, Nottingham and Cambridge.

urban design The collaborative process of shaping the setting for life in cities, towns and villages.

There is at last a general understanding that making places socially, economically and environmentally successful depends on high standards of urban design. What is less understood is how good design can be delivered. The challenge is to influence the development process, not only on high-profile sites but wherever urban change is reshaping places.

Local authorities need a framework of planning and design policy (currently set out in their development plans) complementing the new generation of community plans and neighbourhood renewal strategies. The effectiveness of all of these tools in delivering effective planning and good design depends on urban design guidance, such as urban design frameworks, development briefs and master plans.

There is, though, a great deal of confusion about what design guidance is, how it should be prepared, what clients expect, what services consultants offer, and what resources are required. The aim of this guide is to help people use the right tools for the job, and to use them effectively. It is addressed to everyone who plays a part in commissioning, preparing or using guidance, whether as developers, council officers, consultants, politicians or members of partnerships.

URBAN D...NCE

Urban design fra... ...d master plans

Avril Robarts LRC

Liverpool John Moores University

LIVERPOOL JOHN MOORES UNIVERSITY

ROBERT COWAN

FOREWORD BY JON ROUSE

WITHDRAWN

Urban Design Alliance

URBAN
DESIGN
GROUP

LIVERPOOL JMU LIBRARY

3 1111 01024 7151

Published by Thomas Telford Publishing, Thomas Telford Ltd, 1 Heron Quay, London E14 4JD.
URL: http://www.thomastelford.com

Distributors for Thomas Telford books are
USA: ASCE Press, 1801 Alexander Bell Drive, Reston, VA 20191-4400, USA
Japan: Maruzen Co. Ltd, Book Department, 3–10 Nihonbashi 2-chome, Chuo-ku, Tokyo 103
Australia: DA Books and Journals, 648 Whitehorse Road, Mitcham 3132, Victoria

First published 2002

A catalogue record for this book is available from the British Library

ISBN: 0 7277 3135 1

© Author and Thomas Telford Limited 2002

All rights, including translation, reserved. Except as permitted by the Copyright, Designs and
Patents Act 1988, no part of this publication may be reproduced, stored in a retrieval system
or transmitted in any form or by any means, electronic, mechanical, photocopying or
otherwise, without the prior written permission of the Publishing Director, Thomas Telford
Publishing, Thomas Telford Ltd, 1 Heron Quay, London E14 4JD.

This book is published on the understanding that the author is solely responsible for the
statements made and opinions expressed in it and that its publication does not necessarily
imply that such statements and/or opinions are or reflect the views or opinions of the
publishers. While every effort has been made to ensure that the statements made and the
opinions expressed in this publication provide a safe and accurate guide, no liability or
responsibility can be accepted in this respect by the author or publishers.

Designed and typeset by Kneath Associates, Swansea
Printed and bound in Great Britain by Latimer Trend, Plymouth

Contents

Acknowledgements

The Urban Design Group is grateful to the following for their advice and comments:

Richard Alvey, WS Atkins

Faraz Baber, RICS

Chris Brown, Igloo

John Billingham, *Urban Design Quarterly*

Kelvin Campbell, Urban Initiatives

Roger Evans, Roger Evans Associates

Andrew Gibbins, CityID

Stephen Haines, Leicester City Council

Simon Harrison, Bruce and Partners; Head of Planning and Development Faculty, RICS Scotland

Sebastian Loew, *Urban Design Quarterly*

Paul Murrain, Urban Initiatives

Peter Neal, Prince's Foundation

John Punter, University of Cardiff

Antony Rifkind, Town Centres Ltd

Richard Riley, Leicester City Council

Jon Rowland, Jon Rowland Urban Design

Judith Ryser, Cityscope Europe

Barry Sellars, Wandsworth Borough Council

Nigel Wakefield, WS Atkins

Marcus Wilshere, Urban Initiatives

This guide in no way purports to be either exclusive or exhaustive. The Urban Design Group does not accept any liability for any action arising from the use to which it may be put.

The guide applies specifically to England and Wales.

The Urban Design Group, founded in 1978, is a membership organisation whose aim is to promote effective action in improving towns and cities. See p66 for details of the group and how to join.

Robert Cowan is director of the Urban Design Group and a consultant. He was joint leader of the team at Urban Initiatives on whose work *By Design: urban design in the planning system* (DETR and CABE, 2000) was based, and author of *Designing Places: a policy statement for Scotland* (Scottish Executive, 2001). He is a senior research fellow in the department of architecture at De Montfort University, and an external examiner at the Bartlett School (University College London) and the University of Manchester. His publications include *The Cities Design Forgot* and *The Connected City*.

Foreword

Following the publication of the Green Paper on Planning at the end of 2001, urban design frameworks, development briefs and master plans – indeed, any form of detailed spatial design guidance – have taken on greater significance. This approach follows up one of the key messages of the Urban Task Force, that developing spatial master plans (defined in their report as three-dimensional frameworks of buildings and public spaces) was the fundamental building block to achieving design-led regeneration.

It is an approach that CABE (Commission for Architecture and the Built Environment) supports wholeheartedly. We are the national champion for better places: places that work better, feel better, are better. We offer advice to all those who create, manage and use buildings and the spaces between them.

Our work around the country – and to date CABE's Enabling Programme has been directly advising on around 15 master plans a year, in addition to the almost 100 schemes that come before the Design Review Committee annually – has convinced us of the need for a publication such as this. So we welcome the Urban Design Group's timely contribution.

The advice found on these pages is the latest in a series of complementary guidance that stresses the importance of urban design in the planning system. The joint Department of Transport, Local Government and the Regions DTLR/CABE publication *By Design* sets out the need for better urban design and discusses the key principles for the preparation of site-specific urban design guidance in a wider context. This new contribution builds on the advice in *By Design* by focusing on the detail, and spelling out exactly what local authorities might include in urban design guidance, and what developers and designers should expect to find in it. Hopefully, the result will be less confusion all round and a better quality built environment.

We at CABE share with the Urban Design Group a belief in the power of planning that is proactive rather than reactive. We both believe that quality and innovation are dependent on the calibre and competency of early decision-makers in demanding the best and encouraging its attainment. *Urban Design Guidance* makes this more likely by providing a framework for all those involved in the development process to once again make positive, plan-led planning the norm.

Jon Rouse
Chief Executive
Commission for Architecture and the Built Environment

Introduction

The role of urban design guidance

Government policy has given new importance to urban design through the DTLR/CABE guide *By Design* and the Scottish Executive's *Designing Places*, among many other documents. A consistent theme is the importance of urban design guidance. This has been underlined in the DTLR's green paper *Planning: delivering a fundamental change*.

Urban design guidance is a generic term for documents that guide developers and their designers (and other agents) in planning and designing development. It can be prepared by local authorities, landowners, developers, partnerships, and business and community organisations (all of whom should be involved in the process), or by several of these jointly.

Urban design guidance can support planning policy, facilitate collaboration, express vision, set design standards and indicate the next steps.

Policy
Urban design guidance can:

- allow public policy to set the framework for urban design without becoming involved in an inappropriate level of detail
- provide a framework for development control, relating the council's policies to a particular area or site
- contribute to the process of reviewing the local authority's plans and policies.

Collaboration
Urban design guidance can:

- reflect the views and values of all stakeholders, including local people
- provide a clear basis for dialogue or negotiation between a local authority, partnership, developer, local people and other interests
- save time and effort in negotiating amendments to a planning application
- provide a means for establishing consensus and support.

The future use of any development site is subject to conflicting interests. The process of preparing urban design guidance can help to resolve them.

Vision

Urban design guidance can:

- express a coherent vision of how an area or site can be developed
- provide a degree of certainty about what the local authority, partnership and other agencies will require from developers
- create greater awareness of commercial and practical aspects of a development proposal, and its potential contribution to the local economy, early in the process
- provide a basis for assessing the value of sites
- support the process of assembling development land.

Design standards

Urban design guidance can:

- describe and illustrate the proposed urban form in three dimensions, explaining how that form will achieve the intended vision for the place
- provide the information on which successful development and high standards of design depend
- inspire better and more imaginative architecture by initiating a creative response to the site
- provide a design concept to coordinate the design of individual sites or buildings
- test alternative design and development scenarios
- educate professionals and the public in the value of good design.

Next steps

Urban design guidance can:

- provide a basis for producing more detailed guidance. Urban design frameworks can be followed by development briefs or streetscape manuals, for example
- help in promoting and marketing an area or site
- provide the basis for bidding for public sector funds and securing private sector support
- provide a common basis for comparing developers' proposals.

Carrying out a Placecheck: one way in which local residents can contribute to a site and context appraisal.

Types of urban design guidance

There are four types of guidance that can usually be distinguished from one another.

- Guidance relating to specific places. There are three main types of these: urban design frameworks (for areas), development briefs (for sites) and master plans (for sites).
- Guidance relating to specific topics. These, usually called design guides, cover topics such as shopfronts, house extensions, lighting and cycling.
- Guidance relating to specific policies. Examples are policies on conservation areas, transport corridors, waterfronts, promenades and green belts.
- Guidance relating to a whole local authority area. These may give general urban design guidance for the whole district or county.

This guide focuses on the first of those categories: guidance relating to specific places. Much of it, though, is also relevant to the other types.

Urban design frameworks

- An urban design framework is a document describing and illustrating how planning and design policies and principles should be implemented in an area where there is a need to control, guide and promote change. It includes a two-dimensional vision of future infrastructure requirements.
- Such areas include urban quarters, transport interchanges and corridors, regeneration areas, town centres, urban edges, housing estates, conservation areas, villages, new settlements, urban areas of special landscape value, and suburban areas identified as being suitable for more intense development.
- The area may be one that is likely to be developed in several phases and by several developers.
- An urban design framework often covers an area only part of which is likely to be developed in the near future.
- Urban design frameworks are used to coordinate more detailed development briefs and master plans.
- These frameworks are also called a confusing variety of other names, including urban design strategy, area development framework, and planning and urban design framework.

Development briefs

- A development brief is a document providing guidance on how a specific site of significant size or sensitivity should be developed in line with the relevant planning and design policies. It will usually contain some indicative, but flexible, vision of future development form.
- A development brief usually covers a site most of which is likely to be developed in the near future.
- The terms 'planning brief' and 'design brief' are also sometimes used. These came into use at a time when government policy was that planning and design should be kept separate in design guidance. The term 'development brief' avoids that unworkable distinction.

Master plans

- A master plan is a document that charts the masterplanning process and explains how a site or a series of sites will be developed. It will describe how the proposal will be implemented, and set out the costs, phasing and timing of development.
- A master plan will usually be prepared by or on behalf of an organisation that owns the site or controls the development process.
- As with all design guidance, the purpose of a master plan is to set out principles on matters of importance, not to prescribe in detail how development should be designed. But a master plan should show in some detail how the principles are to be implemented. If the master plan shows an area designated for mixed-use development, for example, it should show a layout that will support such uses (for example by ensuring that the footprints of the buildings are appropriate to the envisaged uses).

The term 'master plan' is used, confusingly, to mean a wide variety of different things. *By Design* (DTLR/CABE, 2000) did not use it at all. *Towards an Urban*

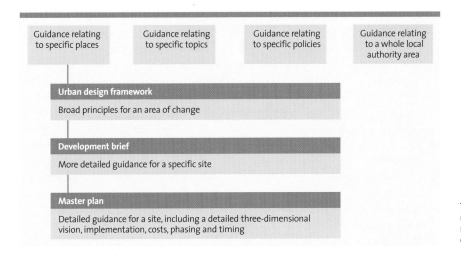

| Guidance relating to specific places | Guidance relating to specific topics | Guidance relating to specific policies | Guidance relating to a whole local authority area |

Urban design framework

Broad principles for an area of change

Development brief

More detailed guidance for a specific site

Master plan

Detailed guidance for a site, including a detailed three-dimensional vision, implementation, costs, phasing and timing

This guide focuses on guidance relating to specific locations, though much of it is relevant also to the other three types.

Types of design guidance	Relates to an area of change	Relates to a specific site	Includes a context appraisal, policy review, vision statement, and planning and design principles	Includes a feasibility appraisal and describes the proposed development process	Includes details of how the proposal will be implemented, and sets out the costs, phasing and timing of development	Usually prepared by or on behalf of an organis-ation that owns the site or controls the development process	Outlines appropriate planning obligations
Urban design framework	■		■	■			■
Development brief		■	■	■			■
Master plan		■	■	■	■	■	■

Characteristics of the types of urban design guidance covered in this guide.

Renaissance, the report of the Urban Task Force (1999), saw master plans as a means of focusing on the visual impact of three-dimensional form. This present guide defines master plans as having a role that is distinct from other forms of guidance, rather than (as happens frequently these days) using master plan as a vague, generic term for a wide variety of types of guidance. Our use of the term is consistent with government policy and acceptable to leading practitioners.

Models can help non-specialists get to grips with an area's planning and design issues in the process of preparing guidance. This one is at Hackney's Building Exploratory.

When guidance is needed: size and complexity

Design guidance (an urban design framework or a development brief) should be provided for any area or site where resolving conflicting objectives is likely to be unusually difficult. In some cases this may be any area or site with more than one owner.

An *urban design framework* should be provided for:

- any area identified in a development plan as requiring an urban design framework
- any area of significant change requiring coordinated action.

A *development brief* should be provided for:

- any site identified in a development plan or an urban design framework as requiring a development brief
- any site of a size specified by a council in its development plan (or elsewhere) as requiring urban design guidance. The size may be specified in terms of area (e.g. one hectare or more) or extent (e.g. an area occupying more than one street block)
- any site subject to development proposals that significantly conflict with local authority policy or standards
- sites for major developments (which may not necessarily be large sites), such as tall buildings or transport interchanges
- sites with specialised design requirements or where planning obligation requirements need to be made explicit.

Site, area and feasibility appraisals will help determine what kind of guidance is required.

Formal status

Urban design guidance can have the status of supplementary planning guidance (SPG) if it is consistent with the development plan; if it has been prepared in consultation with the public, and if the local planning authority has formally adopted it.

Planning inspectors and the Secretary of State for Transport, Local Government and the Regions will give 'substantial' weight to supplementary planning guidance as a *material consideration* in making planning decisions at appeal (or after an application has been 'called in' by the Secretary of State).

The government insists that SPG must be consistent with national and regional planning guidance, as well as with the policies set out in the adopted development plan. It should be clearly cross-referenced to the relevant plan policy or proposal that it supplements. It should be issued separately from the plan and made publicly available. Consultation should be carried out, and the status of SPG should be made clear. SPG should be reviewed regularly alongside reviews of the development plan policies or proposals to which it relates.

Design codes

A design code is a document (with detailed drawings or diagrams) setting out with some precision how the design and planning principles should be applied to development in a particular place. A design code may be included as part of an urban design framework, a development brief or a master plan when a degree of prescription is appropriate. Preparing a design code requires a high degree of skill, and this present guide does not describe how to do it.

Design statements

Design statements complement design guidance in the planning process. A developer makes a *pre-application design statement* to explain the design principles on which a development proposal in progress is based. It enables the local authority to give an initial response to the main issues raised by the proposal. An applicant for planning permission submits a *planning application design statement* with the application, setting out the design principles adopted in relation to the site and its wider context. Government advice (Planning Policy Guidance Note 1) encourages an applicant for planning permission to submit such a written statement to the local authority.

A design statement should explain and illustrate the design principles and design concept; outline how these will be reflected in the development's layout, density, scale, landscape and visual appearance; provide a well-considered rationale for the design, based on the characteristics of the site and its wider area (through a full site and area appraisal where appropriate), and to the purpose of the proposed development; and explain how the development will meet the local authority's planning and urban design objectives. The content of the design statement mirrors that of a development brief or other guidance. This means that a developer who has helped in preparing a brief will find that much of the work involved in preparing the design statement has already been done.

The UDG intends to provide further guidance on design statements in a later publication.

Preparing and using guidance

Public involvement

Involving stakeholders and a wider public in the planning process in a meaningful way at an early stage is essential. Too often local authorities, partnerships and developers provide an opportunity to get involved that makes little sense in relation to the timing and substance of the development process. The result is unnecessary frustration and delay for everyone. The process of preparing urban design guidance can provide an opportunity for structured public involvement, involving the right people at the right time. The process needs to be carefully planned from the start, ensuring that the necessary skills and resources are made available.

Effective urban design guidance brings together the perspectives of people who may have a range of conflicting interests. Policy-makers, regulators and controllers set out a series of official requirements. People who live or work locally, and others who carry out professional appraisals, bring an understanding of the local context. Developers, landowners, property agents and development agencies focus on the implications of market conditions. Planners, urban designers, architects, landscape architects, engineers and project managers, among many other professionals, have their own particular approaches to managing the design and development process.

No one is too young to start thinking about what sort of place they would like to live in.

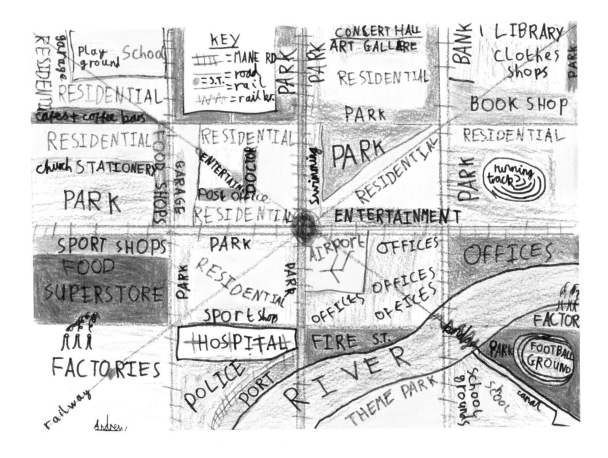

The guidance document, and its various drafts, should set out what has been understood, and express conclusions in a form to which people can agree. A structure such as that of the checklist in this present guide can provide a comprehensive format, tailored to local conditions, for the design and planning process itself. The quality of the public involvement will play a major part in determining the usefulness of the guidance. Preparing urban design guidance at arms' length from the people on the receiving end may save time and money, but it produces guidance that soon proves to be of no use at all in the real world.

A wide range of people may need to become involved in appraising the site and context, creating the vision, drawing up planning and design principles, drawing up options based on those principles, and evaluating the options. In recent years a great deal of experience has been built up in how to manage this process. Nick Wates' *Community Planning Handbook*, for example, describes more than 50 methods of participation that might be appropriate for a particular programme of public involvement. (The handbook is available from the Urban Design Group, price £5 – normal price £14.95.)

Explaining the process

A local authority should specify in the development plan or in guidance documents:

- what degree of detail (what scale of drawings, for example) will be expected in urban design frameworks, development briefs and master plans at different stages in the planning process
- what pre-application discussions will be required
- what information will be required as part of the planning application

The process of preparing guidance can structure the process of collaborative planning.

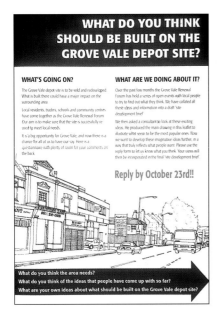

- any policies which apply to particular areas or sites, and which will be the starting point for guidance
- which particular sites should have guidance with the status of supplementary planning guidance
- the criteria (relating to scale, for example) that will determine which other sites (not yet identified) should have development briefs with the status of supplementary planning guidance
- how urban design guidance should be prepared. (Different procedures may be appropriate for briefs prepared by the local authority, or jointly between the local authority and another organisation, such as a partnership, landowner, developer, town centre management initiative, amenity society or community group.)

A local authority that does not have the necessary skills and resources to guide people through the process in this way should at least be actively considering how to obtain them.

Resources

Allocating resources to prepare urban design guidance should pay dividends. The guidance itself can help to release resources, through showing what quality of development might be achieved or through benefits derived from planning obligations, for example. Local authorities, developers, landowners and everyone else involved in the development process know the cost in time and money of the uncertainty, misunderstanding, confusion and delay caused by ill-conceived development proposals and inadequately prepared planning authorities. Avoiding protracted planning applications, planning appeals and public inquiries is worth a great deal.

It is almost always worthwhile to spend time and resources in involving a wide range of people in preparing guidance.

How much work is involved in preparing guidance will depend on the scale and sensitivity of the area or site and of any likely development. At the lowest level, a development brief for a small gap site may require no more than simple guidance about such matters as height, access, the building line and materials, and consultation with neighbours. At the other extreme, an urban design framework or brief for a site on which major development is expected will require comprehensive assessments of complex issues, and extensive consultation.

In all cases, the effectiveness of the guidance will depend on the quality of the appraisals of context and feasibility.

Although development briefs should be prepared individually and tailored to the particular site, it may be appropriate for several briefs to share a common structure and certain important elements. This can save time and work.

The right time

As a tool of dynamic planning, urban design guidance is effective only if it relates to markets, programmes and attitudes as they are at a particular time (while being flexible enough to accommodate a degree of change). Guidance may need to be updated to make sure of this.

Some guidance is prepared too late, when landowners and prospective developers have already decided what they want to build and are reluctant to rethink their ideas. A developer who has bought land on the assumption that its value will be enhanced by a particular form of development is unlikely to agree to be bound by guidance that will prevent that value from being realised. Local authorities need to prepare guidance in advance of interest being expressed in a site, so that their planning and design requirements are reflected in the price paid for the land.

A local authority should encourage landowners and developers to prepare design guidance (in partnership with the council if possible) at the moment when they are beginning to think about how sites might be developed. Their incentive should be a streamlined and more certain planning process.

Development plan revisions often provide an ideal time to set out planning and design principles for major development sites. This can be done more easily if thoroughgoing capacity studies are carried out.

Changing the guidance

A guidance document can be altered or replaced if conditions change. A further process of collaboration and consultation may be necessary to define and respond to those new conditions, and the revised guidance may need to be re-adopted by the local authority to give it the status of supplementary planning guidance.

The right skills

If the skills are not available within a local authority to produce urban design frameworks and development briefs, the council may well not be up to negotiating with developers about design issues or assessing the design merits of planning applications. It may be appropriate to commission external urban design consultants for specific tasks if design skills are not available among the council's staff.

The quality and value of the guidance will be greatly enhanced by skills of planning and urban design. What is appropriate, and whether or not particular specialists are needed, will depend on the nature and complexity of the place and its circumstances.

If the local authority lacks design capability, a developer can be asked to treat the initial stages of the design of a development as part of the process of preparing an urban design guidance document. The basic design principles can then be evolved openly, systematically and, in collaboration with the developer, benefiting from the certainty that approved guidance offers.

Preparing urban design guidance is likely to require creative collaboration from a wide range of skilled people. These people will include those who interpret policy; assess the local economy and property market; appraise a site or area in terms of land use, ecology, landscape, ground conditions, social factors, history, archaeology, urban form and transport; manage and facilitate a participative process; draft and illustrate design principles; and programme the development process. Those who take the lead in this work should be skilled in promoting collaboration among, not just professionals, but everyone who has a hand in shaping places.

Local authorities need to ensure that their awareness of, and skills in, urban design extend to policy makers, development controllers, regulators and elected members.

Effective guidance draws on large amounts of information, but is itself succinct, clearly written and logically structured. A short guidance document can take more time and skill to write than a long one.

Government research on the preparation of development briefs concluded that it was better to produce no design guidance at all than guidance that was poorly related to the local context and circumstances.

Illustrating the planning and design criteria

Drawing skills are valuable in preparing guidance. Firstly, the act of drawing can be part of a designer's creative process. Secondly, drawings can help to communicate ideas during the collaborative process of exploring options. Thirdly, drawings can help to explain the guidance to its users.

Designers who prepare guidance are sometimes tempted to design a building or buildings that would conform to the principles, and to include the worked-up drawings in the guidance. This may confuse potential developers, who will not easily be able to tell which aspects of the drawings illustrate the application of the principles, and which have been included merely to enhance the guide's appearance.

Concept diagrams, analytic diagrams, building envelope guidelines (diagrams with dimensions), and three-dimensional sketches of building forms and spaces can all be used to show how the guidance's planning and design criteria might be applied. Illustrations of buildings and spaces in other places can also help to communicate ideas without prescribing exactly what to design.

Using the guidance

The effectiveness of the guidance will depend on council officers (development control planners as well as urban designers) and councillors being committed to it, and using it as a basis for their discussions and negotiations with developers, and for decisions on planning applications. This commitment can be built by involving these people in preparing the guidance, and by the council organising seminars for councillors and officers on particular guidance and on the use of guidance in general.

The local authority must also involve the same people in monitoring the quality of what gets built, and reviewing the urban design guidance in the light of it.

Enforcement

Guidance is not enforceable directly unless the local authority has a stake in the land or is co-financing the development, but the council's requirements can be made enforceable by various means. These include conditions in a planning permission; covenants in a building agreement or land disposal; planning agreements under Section 106 of the Town and Country Planning Act 1990; or other powers available to local authorities for non-planning matters.

This framework set the brief for a developer competition for a site at King's Dock, Liverpool. The mixed-use development is centred on a sports stadium.

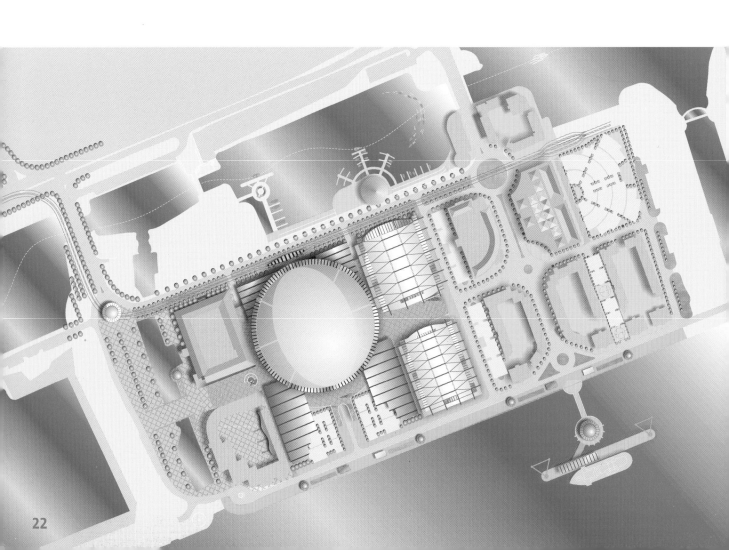

Selected further reading

Civic Trust and English Historic Towns Forum (1993) *Traffic Measures in Historic Towns*.

DETR (1998) *Places, Streets and Movement: a companion guide to Design Bulletin 32*.

DETR and CABE (2000) *By Design: urban design in the planning system, towards better practice*, Thomas Telford Publishing.

DTLR *Transport: a guide to better practice*, PPG 13.

DTLR (2001) *Planning: delivering a fundamental change* (green paper).

DTLR and CABE (2001) *Better Places to Live: a companion guide to PPG3*, Thomas Telford Publishing.

DTLR and CABE (2001) *The Value of Urban Design*, Thomas Telford Publishing.

DTLR and CABE (2001) *Urban Design Skills Working Group*.

Llewelyn-Davies (2000) *Urban Design Compendium*, English Partnerships and the Housing Corporation, London.

Punter, J. and Carmona, M. (1997) *The Design Dimension of Planning: theory, content and best practice for design policies*, E and FN Spon, London.

Scottish Executive (2001) *Designing Places*.

Wates, N. (2000) *Community Planning Handbook*, Earthscan.

Note
The DETR's *Planning and Development Briefs: a guide to better practice*, published in 1998, has been overtaken by subsequent guidance (particularly *By Design*) and practice.

LIVERPOOL JOHN MOORES UNIVERSITY
Aldham Roberts L.R.C.
TEL. 051 231 3701/3634

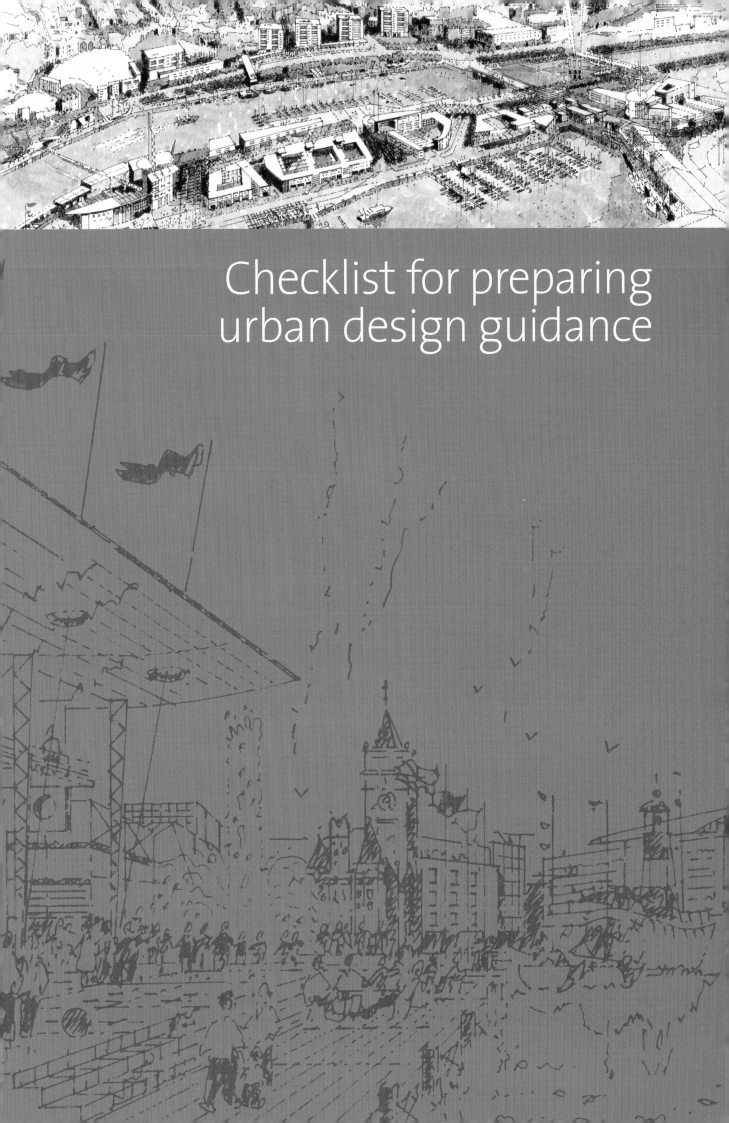

Checklist for preparing urban design guidance

Checklist for preparing urban design guidance

What kind of guidance?

To find out what kind of planning and urban design guidance is appropriate, and what kind of information, guidance and illustrative material the document should contain, those preparing or commissioning it should ask:

- What is the purpose of the guidance?
- Who is it intended for?
- How does it fit into the planning and development process in relation to that particular site or area?
- How large or complex is the area or site?
- What resources and skills are needed to prepare it?
- How will it be used?
- How will it relate to other existing or proposed guidance?

First steps

The first step is to establish the process of preparing the guidance. This will involve asking:

- Who needs to be involved in preparing the guidance?
- In the case of guidance prepared jointly by different organisations, who will undertake the initial work of preparing each of its sections?
- What appraisals need to be carried out? (Where the guidance is to be supplementary planning guidance, the local authority will need to approve any appraisals that it does not carry out itself.)
- What will be the timetable for preparing the guidance?
- What processes of collaboration and consultation will be used?
- How will differences of interpretation and conflicts of interest be resolved?
- What process will lead to the local authority adopting the guidance?

Using the checklist

This checklist presents an outline for a possible urban design guidance document. It will help in choosing priorities and making sure nothing of importance has been forgotten. It is not a list of contents that must be covered fully and comprehensively. Guidance will never cover all the matters listed here: it should set out only what is important in relation to the place and to the guidance's purpose. Following the checklist's structure will not guarantee that the urban design guidance draws the right conclusions, but it will help to make it comprehensive.

All urban design frameworks, development briefs and master plans should generally
include the following sections:

- vision statement
- site and context appraisal
- policy review
- feasibility appraisal
- planning and design principles
- indicative design concepts and proposals
- details of the proposed development process.

In addition, a master plan should generally also include:

- details of how the proposal will be implemented
- details of costs, phasing and timing of development.

**An initial concept sketch in
watercolour of a proposed mixed-use
development on the River Thames at
Thamesmead. The edge of the
existing town centre appears in the
foreground.**

Vision

This section comes at the start of the document as a concise statement of its main idea, with illustrations where appropriate. Creating the vision, though, will not be the first step in preparing the guidance. Appraising the site and context, for one, will precede it.

Summarise

What vision of the future of the place has inspired this guidance?
The vision will be developed through a process of appraisals, consultation and collaboration, and creative thinking about planning and design principles. The process may involve any of the methods of planning and urban design, and in particular techniques of vision-building (see *The Community Planning Handbook* by Nick Wates, available from the Urban Design Group. See p66).

Particularly in illustrating the vision, the document should make clear whether these are ideas for which the costings, phasing, timing and implementation have been worked out, or if these are merely visualisations of some initial ideas about what the place could become.

What sort of place should this become?

- What key words or phrases describe the qualities that it is hoped development will achieve?
- What character and uses would achieve these qualities?
- What timescale is the guidance looking to: temporary uses, short-term uses, or long term (perhaps even 100 years)?

What objectives should development aim for, and which of them are most important?

Left A clear vision of before and after.

Right A vision of how the physical form of Poole could develop.

Left Using Planning for Real to decide priorities for change. Centre A sketch gives an impression of what a new space might feel like. Right A vision of Cardiff Bay's inner harbour. Below An impression of what new development in Boulogne might look like.

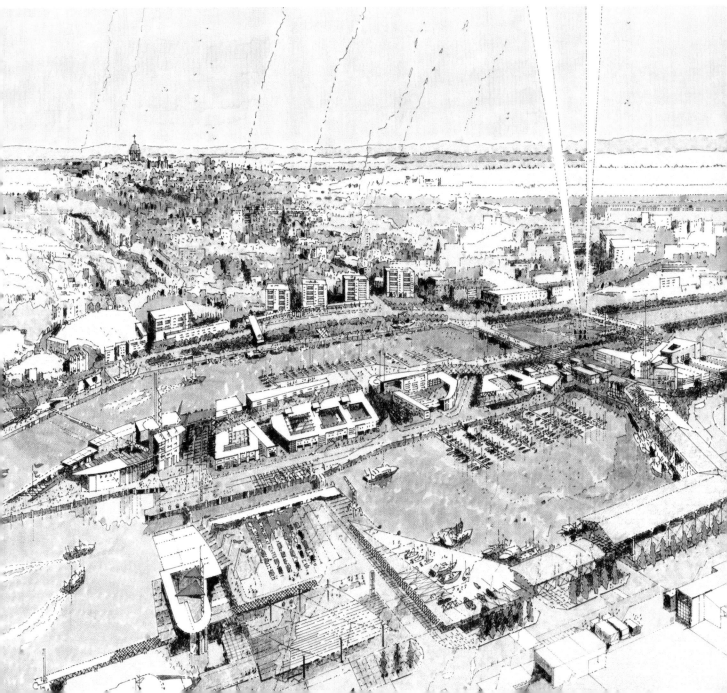

Background

The area or site

What are the boundaries of the area or site?

- Include references to site and location plans.

Purpose of the guidance

Why has the guidance been prepared?

There may be several reasons, such as to:

- satisfy a requirement by the local authority that guidance should be prepared for every site of a certain size or significant complexity
- provide a starting point for dialogue or negotiation with developers
- evolve a shared vision
- build consensus for action
- tackle particular problems that the place presents
- respond to development pressures
- promote high standards of design
- identify development opportunities
- promote and market the area or site
- provide a framework for development control
- contribute to the process of preparing or reviewing a development plan in circumstances where the existing plan does not provide an adequate policy context
- support the process of assembling development land
- provide the basis for bidding for public sector funds and securing private sector support
- educate council officers and members, and other users.

Roles and responsibilities

Who has prepared the guidance?

Who will be responsible for various aspects of making sure that the guidance is used as intended?

Date of publication

When was this version of the guidance adopted/published?

Status: draft, or approved as supplementary planning guidance

Is this version of the guidance a draft (if so, which draft)?

Has this version been approved by the local authority as supplementary planning guidance (SPG)?

- See 'Formal status', p15.

If not, is it intended that it will be approved as SPG later?

Policy review

What policies and guidance apply, and how should they be interpreted in relation to this area or site?

National and regional planning policy and guidance

What national and regional policy and guidance is particularly relevant here?

Relevant policy and guidance may be contained in or relate to:

- planning policy guidance notes (PPGs, issued by the Secretary of State for Transport, Local Government and the Regions)
- regional planning guidance (RPGs, also issued by the Secretary of State)
- the regional development agency.

Policies and requirements of public bodies

What requirements of other public bodies need to be taken into account?

Relevant bodies might include:

- Regional development agency
- Countryside Agency
- English Heritage
- English Partnerships
- Environment Agency
- Government office
- Police authority.

Development plan policies

Which of the local authority's planning policies apply to the area or site?

Every place is covered either by a 'unitary development plan' or by a development plan comprising more than one document (a structure plan and a local plan, and sometimes also other plans relating to minerals and waste).

Refer to the policies or quote them, as appropriate. Relevant policies may cover, among other things:

- land uses
- design
- interim uses
- conservation areas
- listed buildings
- ancient monuments
- archaeology
- Sites of Special Scientific Interest
- local nature reserves and other designated ecological sites
- protected flora and fauna
- nature conservation, countryside and green strategies
- airport protection zones.

Other local authority policies and standards

Are other local authority policies or standards relevant to development here?

These might relate to:

- highways
- parking
- housing
- environmental health
- education
- leisure
- strategic views.

Urban design framework and development briefs

If the guidance is a development brief or a master plan, is the site covered by an urban design framework?

If it is a master plan, is there a relevant development brief?

A plan showing policies and local conditions relating to a development site.

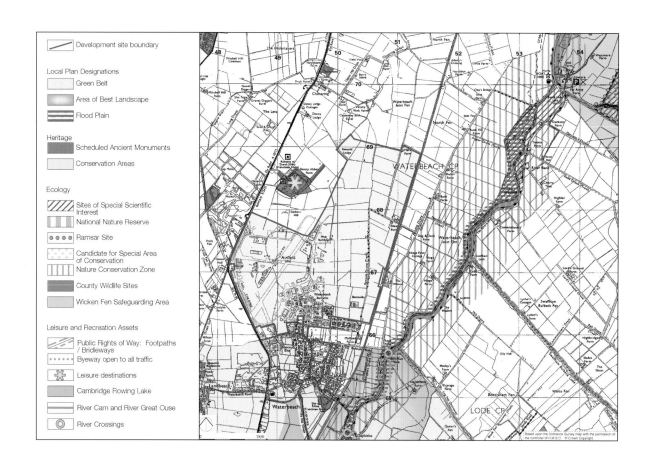

Development site boundary

Local Plan Designations
Green Belt
Area of Best Landscape
Flood Plain

Heritage
Scheduled Ancient Monuments
Conservation Areas

Ecology
Sites of Special Scientific Interest
National Nature Reserve
Ramsar Site
Candidate for Special Area of Conservation
Nature Conservation Zone
County Wildlife Sites
Wicken Fen Safeguarding Area

Leisure and Recreation Assets
Public Rights of Way: Footpaths / Bridleways
Byeway open to all traffic
Leisure destinations
Cambridge Rowing Lake
River Cam and River Great Ouse
River Crossings

Design guides

Do any design guides apply to the place?

A design guide is a document providing guidance on how development can be carried out in accordance with the design policies of a local authority or other organisation. Design guides are issued by some counties (covering issues such as residential development, roads and vernacular style) and by many district and unitary authorities (covering many types and aspects of development, such as shopfronts, house extensions and satellite dishes). A design guide can be given weight by being subject to public consultation and by being approved by the council as supplementary planning guidance.

Local design statement

Is the area covered by a local design statement?

Local design statements (as distinct from plain 'design statements', see pxx) include village design statements and Placecheck reports. A village design statement is an advisory document, usually produced by a village community, showing how development can be carried out in harmony with the village and its setting. A local design statement can be given weight by being prepared in consultation with the public and approved by the council as supplementary planning guidance. Placechecks are described in the next section (Site and context appraisal).

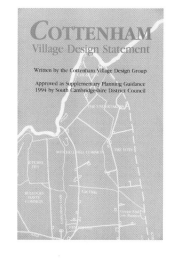

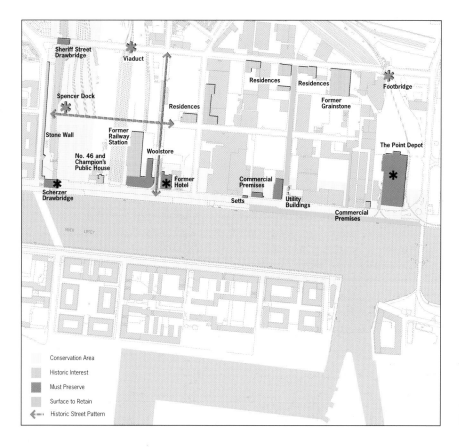

The heritage features of an area of Dublin.

Other supplementary planning guidance

Is the area covered by any other supplementary planning guidance?

Conservation areas

Is the area covered by any conservation area statements or appraisals?

If so, how have these been integrated into or referred to in the guidance?

Local Agenda 21 action plan

Is there a Local Agenda 21 action plan (or other document about sustainable development) relevant to this place?

Local authorities promote sustainable development through Local Agenda 21 action plans (among other means), based on local consultation about the likely impact of development on the social, economic and environmental conditions of people in the future and in other places.

Utilities

What requirements for utilities need to be taken into account?

- Gas
- Electricity
- Water
- Cable

How can utilities be provided in ways that will facilitate the planning and design of development here?

Local initiatives

Are there any local initiatives relevant to the development of the area?

Such initiatives might include:

- design awards
- design competitions
- design initiatives
- design advisory panels or conservation area advisory groups (panels or groups of people with specialist knowledge, which meet regularly or occasionally to advise a local authority or other organisation on the design merits of planning applications, or other planning and design issues)
- architecture and planning centres (an architecture and planning centre is a building which provides a focus for a range of activities and services, such as discussions, information, exhibitions, collaboration and professional services, relating to design and planning).

Planning history of the site or area, including previous planning decisions and results of public consultations

What planning documents are relevant to the area or site?

What previous planning decisions need to be taken into account?

Have any public consultations been carried out in relation to the area or site?
If so, what were the results?

Legal rights and restrictions, including covenants and easements

Do any legal rights and restrictions apply?

These might include:

- conservation areas
- listed buildings
- covenants
- easements
- rights of way and access
- rights of light
- tree preservation orders
- ransom strips held by landowners.

Diagram showing the strategic development potential for Kent Thames-side.

LIVERPOOL JOHN MOORES UNIVERSITY

Site and context appraisal

What aspects of the place should be taken into account in planning and designing development?

A large variety of methods of site and context appraisal is available. Many of them can be used to involve the public and a wide range of stakeholders in preparing design guidance. The following are a few of the methods.

- The Placecheck method (developed by the Urban Design Alliance) assesses the qualities of a place, showing what improvements are needed, and focusing people on working together to achieve them. A Placecheck can cover a street (or part of one), a neighbourhood, a town centre, or a whole district or city. The *Placecheck Users' Guide* can be downloaded from **www.placecheck.com**.
- SWOT (strengths, weaknesses, opportunities and threats) analysis is a common way of considering some basic questions about a place.
- Space syntax analysis is a technique for analysing movement through urban space and predicting the amount of activity likely to result from that movement. A checklist for assessing how street clutter can be reduced is provided in *Traffic Measures in Historic Towns* (Civic Trust and English Historic Towns Forum, 1993).
- A checklist for carrying out an audit of transport conditions in an area is provided in PPG13 *Transport: a guide to better practice* (DTLR).
- Fruin analysis (a method of analysing pedestrian movement devised by John Fruin) can be used to assess levels of comfort on pedestrian routes.
- Lynchian analysis (devised by Kevin Lynch) focuses on such features as gateways, points of transition, nodes, landmarks, views and vistas, and edges, seams and barriers.
- Tissue studies compare the scale and layout of different settlements. The technique makes use of overprinting or tracing maps of successful and familiar places over the proposed development site or area, at the same scale. This provides clues as to the capacity of a place and how it may be structured.

Annotated sketches help to reveal the area's character.

Left An old map sets the area in its historical context. **Right** A diagram shows development opportunities at London's King's Cross.

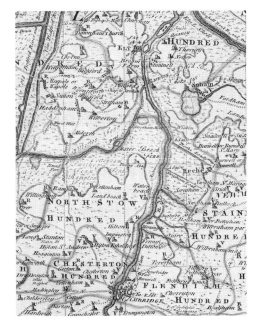

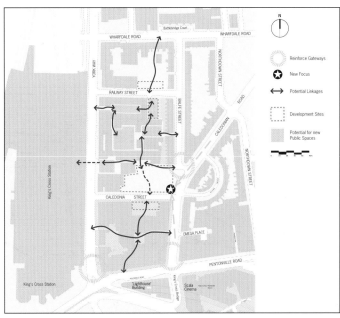

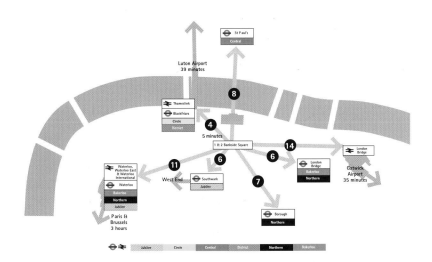

Diagrams showing (above) the transport accessibility of London's Bankside and (below) the wider context of Cork, Ireland.

Plans

What plans are appropriate will depend on the type of guidance. Guidance should always contain the following plans and diagrams:

- Location plan, with North point, scale and Ordnance Survey grid reference.
- Plans of site and surrounding area, with North points, indication of scale of plans and contours or levels.

Historic plans, where these provide useful information about how the area has developed, can be included.

Figure/ground diagrams can be a useful way of showing the relationship between built form and publicly accessible space (including streets) by presenting the former in black and the latter as a white background, or the other way round.

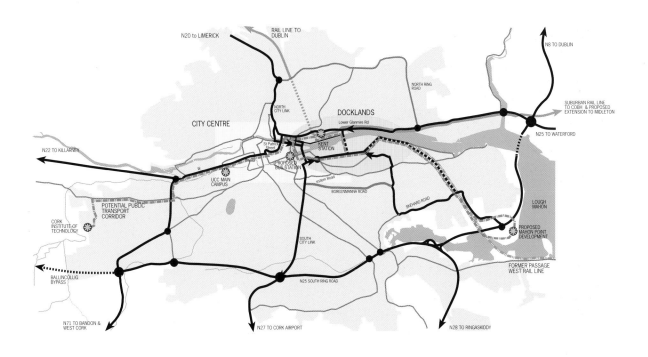

Carrying out Placechecks in Barnsley and Liverpool.

Illustrations of the area

These should include:

- photographs (including aerial)
- drawings (including sections through the site and streets)
- historic drawings and photographs
- context appraisal diagrams (annotated diagrams showing the significance of various features of the area, summarising what the area appraisal describes in greater detail).

Written appraisal

The written appraisal with illustrations will describe the features of the area that are likely to be relevant to development.

Land uses

What is the place used for at present (including informal uses)?

What uses are found in the surrounding area?

In what ways are the existing uses likely to be sensitive to how the place is developed?

Local aspirations

What do people living in the area hope that development will provide?

How do local people use the place now, and how would they like to use it in future?

What other concerns do local people have about the development and the area's future?

Development capacity

What indications are there of how much development the place is likely to be able to accommodate?

Appraising the site and area in terms of urban design objectives

By Design (DTLR/CABE) identifies seven objectives of urban design (character; continuity and enclosure; quality of the public realm; ease of movement; legibility; adaptability; and diversity). These objectives can be used to structure a site and context appraisal, and they provide headings for the checklist below.

Character

NATURAL FEATURES	
Landscape setting and type	What sort of landscape does the place have?
Land form	What is the shape of the land? Where does it rise and fall?
Hydrology	Where is there water and how does it move (including rivers, streams, lakes, ponds, and swampy or floodable ground)?
Geology and soils	What are the soils, sub-soils and rocks?
Ecology and wildlife	What living things (flora and fauna) are to be found on the site and in the area? What do they depend on?
Trees and hedgerows	What trees and hedgerows are to be found here?

■ Location   ■ Species
■ Condition   ■ Size
■ Tree Preservation Orders

Urban design analysis of Kilburn town centre

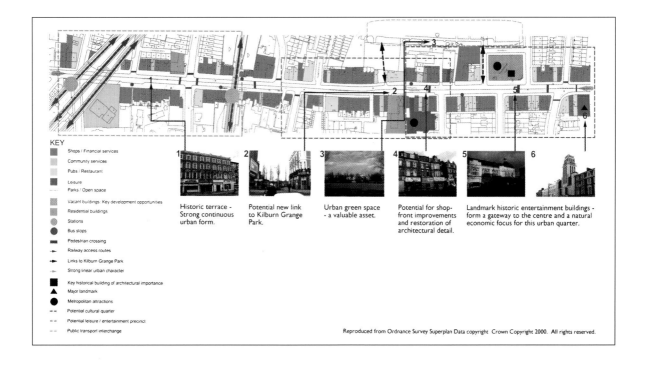

KEY

- Shops / Financial services
- Community services
- Pubs / Restaurant
- Leisure
- Parks / Open space
- Vacant buildings: Key development opportunities
- Residential buildings
- Stations
- Bus stops
- Pedestrian crossing
- Railway access routes
- Links to Kilburn Grange Park
- Strong linear urban character
- Key historical building of architectural importance
- Major landmark
- Metropolitan attractions
- Potential cultural quarter
- Potential leisure / entertainment precinct
- Public transport interchange

1 Historic terrace - Strong continuous urban form.

2 Potential new link to Kilburn Grange Park.

3 Urban green space - a valuable asset.

4 Potential for shop-front improvements and restoration of architectural detail.

5 Landmark historic entertainment buildings - form a gateway to the centre and a natural economic focus for this urban quarter.

6

Reproduced from Ordnance Survey Superplan Data copyright Crown Copyright 2000. All rights reserved.

Climate	What sort of climate does the area have? What are the prevailing winds in summer and winter?
Microclimate	What is the climate like in the area (and in particular parts)? ▓ Exposure to wind and weather ▓ Wind funnels ▓ Cold air drainage channels ▓ Frost pockets ▓ Damp hollows
Orientation	Which way do sites slope or face in relation to the sun?

HUMAN IMPACT

Boundaries	What are the boundaries of the area or site?
Area	What is the area in hectares?
Contamination	Is the ground contaminated? What would be involved in cleaning it up?
Pollution	Is the air or water polluted? What would be involved in purifying it?
Undermining	Has the site been undermined?
Aesthetic quality	What are the area's or site's most visually attractive features?
Noise	Do any parts of the area or site suffer from noise? What would be involved in alleviating it?
Historical development	How did the area and the site develop in the past?
Settlement pattern	What sort of street layout does the area have?
Archaeology	Do any sites need to be investigated (through records or by digging) for possible archaeological value?
Cultural characteristics and heritage	What is distinctive about the way local people live and have lived here in the past?
Local history	What aspects of local history may be relevant to future development?
Events/festivals	What local events and festivals should be taken into account in planning and designing in the area?
Place names	What local place names should be taken into account in planning and designing in the area?
Census data	What information from the census should be taken into account in planning and designing in the area?

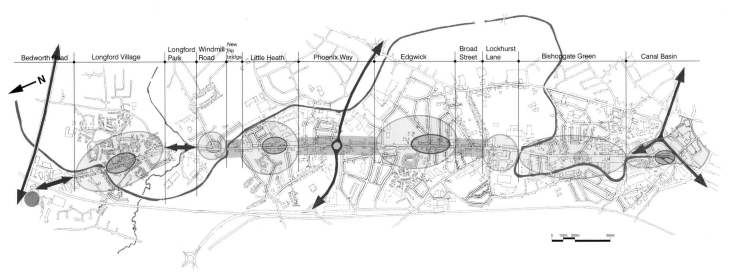

Bedworth Road	Longford Village	Longford Park	Windmill Road	New Inn bridge	Little Heath	Phoenix Way	Edgwick	Broad Street	Lockhurst Lane	Bishopgate Green	Canal Basin

Key

↔ Green corridor
↔ Primary route
▨ Confused area
◯ Character area
◉ District/Neighbourhood centre
◯ Local centre
◉ Character area in need of a 'heart'
● Potential gateway

Diagram showing the potential of a road corridor.

BUILDINGS AND STRUCTURES

Colour and textures	What distinctive colours and textures are found on buildings, structures and surfaces in the area?
Facade treatments	What distinctive types of building front are there in the area?
Building elements and fenestration	What locally distinctive ways are there of using elements of a building such as windows, doors, cornices, string courses, bargeboards, porches and chimneys?
Rhythm and pattern	What regularity and order does the streetscape have?
Details and richness	How are building details and materials used to contribute to the area's interest?
Local/regional building materials	What building materials are used traditionally in the area, and which materials are available in the region?
Local vernacular	In what other traditional ways do or did local builders work?
Age of built fabric	What are the ages of buildings and structures in the area?
Conservation areas	Is any part of the area or site in a conservation area? (English Heritage has published guidance on conservation area character appraisal.)
Listed buildings	Are any buildings or structures listed for their architectural or historical value?

Continuity and enclosure

Continuity	Are the building lines continuous, or do gap sites and abnormal setbacks interrupt them?
Enclosure	How do buildings, structures and natural features contribute to, or detract from, a feeling of enclosure?
Back views	Do any buildings present their backs to public space, including roads?
Active frontages	Are frontages at ground floor level active or dead?

Quality of the public realm

Overlooking	Are public routes and spaces overlooked?
Hard landscaping	What is the quality of workmanship and materials of paving, kerbs, walls, steps and ramps?

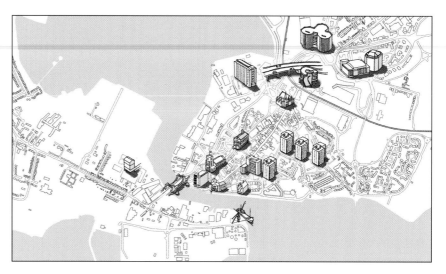

Left Diagram analysing the spaces, pedestrian routes and views of landmarks in a town centre. **Right** A representation of the existing landmarks in Poole town centre.

Planting	What trees, planters, and grassed or planted areas are there?
Street furniture	What signs, seats, bins, bollards, manhole covers, tree grilles and railings are there?
Structures	What bus shelters, kiosks, stalls, information points, pedestrian bridges, beacons and temporary structures are there?
Safety and security	What safety and security facilities (such as closed circuit television) are there?
Maintenance	How easy are publicly accessible places to maintain?

Ease of movement

Public transport	What public transport routes and stops serve the area?
Roads	What is the area's road network?
Access to site	What are the present and potential means of getting to and around the area for vehicles (including bicycles, cars and service vehicles) and pedestrians (including those with potentially restricted mobility)?
Parking	What parking arrangements are there?
Pedestrian routes and flows	Where do people walk on, to or near here? What routes would they like to take if they were available?
Cycling	What facilities for cycling are there?
Transport proposals	What current proposals for roads, footpaths or public transport might be relevant to future development?
Transport assessment	Will a transport assessment be required?
Green travel plans	Will a green travel plan be required?
Air quality	How does the air quality influence movement choices?

Legibility (ease of understanding)

Image and perception	What image, if any, do people (locals and outsiders) have of the place?
Local views	What is visible from particular points on or around the area?
Strategic views	What is visible from particular distant points, and what distant views are there?
Vistas	Are there any notable narrow views past a series of landmarks?
Landmarks	What buildings or structures (on or visible from here) stand out from the background buildings?
Skylines	What buildings (on or visible from here) can be seen against the sky?
Roofscape	What sort of views of roofs are there from (and of) the place?
Gateways	Are there places at the edge of the area or site that are seen (or could potentially be seen) as gateways to it?
Thresholds	Are there places at the edge of (or within) the area or site that are seen (or could potentially be seen) as points where its function or character (or development on it) changes?
Boundaries and barriers	What boundaries and barriers are there at the edge of (or within) the area or site?
Nodes	Where are activity and routes concentrated?

A diagram and sketch from the development brief for the new residential and business community of Swanton Village at Cheeseman's Green, South Ashford, showing the proposed layout and massing.

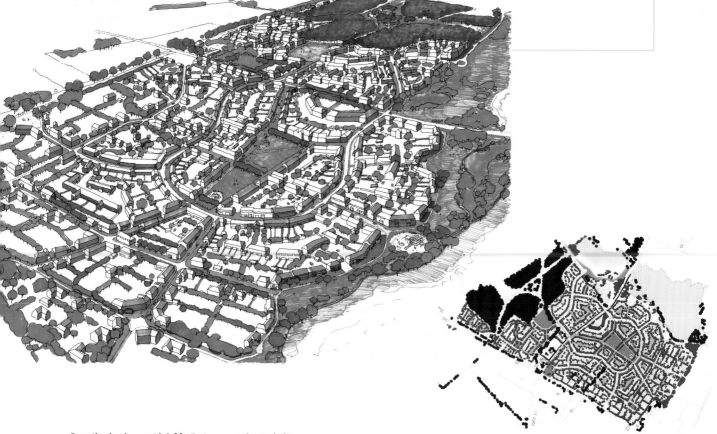

From the development brief for East Stour Village at Cheeseman's Green, South Ashford, showing the proposed layout and massing.

Adaptability

What aspects of the area or site and its existing buildings contribute to its adaptability?

Diversity

What aspects of the area or site and its existing buildings contribute to its potential for diversity and a mix of uses?

Integration and efficiency

What aspects of the area or site and its existing buildings contribute to its potential for using resources efficiently?

Solar energy	What opportunities are there for development to make use of daylight, solar gain, solar panels or photovoltaic technology? What opportunities are there for making use of underground energy sources by means of heat pumps?
Water	What opportunities are there for reducing water run-off and flood risk, and recycling water? What opportunities are there for using aquifers to cool buildings?
Wind	How can the wind be used for ventilation and as an energy source?
Waste	How can the use of non-renewable resources (including energy, land, water and building materials) be minimised?

Does the area or site offer any other opportunities for integrating land use, transport and the natural environment?

Infrastructure and services

Roads	What roads are there on or near the area or site?
Location	Where are any services located here?
Capacity	What is the capacity of any services available? Services may include gas, electricity, water and cable TV.

Feasibility appraisal

What uses are realistic and achievable here in view of economic and market conditions?

Site ownership and tenure

Who owns key sites (in whole or in part)?

Who holds leases or tenancies on these sites (in whole or in part)?

What restrictions are there on legal titles?

Legal rights

What wayleaves and rights of way are there?

Financial implications of aspects of the site and context

What cost implications or revenue benefits are there of issues identified in the site and context appraisal (p36)?

Existing feasibility studies

Are there any existing studies of the feasibility (appropriateness in relation to economic and market conditions) of particular uses here?

If so, what do they say?

Economic and property market appraisal

What do economic conditions suggest are appropriate ways to develop here?

The following may be relevant:

- unemployment rates
- availability or shortages of skills
- employment patterns (who works where?)
- local industries
- shopping patterns (who shops where?).

Does the local property market suggest what is appropriate to develop here?

Examine the following:

- property prices
- rental levels
- amount and type of vacant property.

Sources for this information may include:

- local authority property department
- developers and landowners
- chartered surveyors
- estate agents
- specialist property consultants
- observation.

It is important to note that what the local property market has supported in the past may not be a good guide to what it will support in the future. One of the purposes of design guidance is to encourage all parties in the development process to consider how to build to a higher standard than has previously been achieved locally.

What features of the place are likely to be of particular interest to potential developers or investors in development?

Such features might include:

- physical constraints
- regional context
- demographic issues (how is the population changing?)
- nearby attractions.

Potential developers, development partners and sources of grants

Are any particular developers, investors or potential occupiers known to be interested in the area?

Is anyone in particular likely to be interested in developing here in partnership?

Is a development agency concerned with the area?

What sources of grants are available?

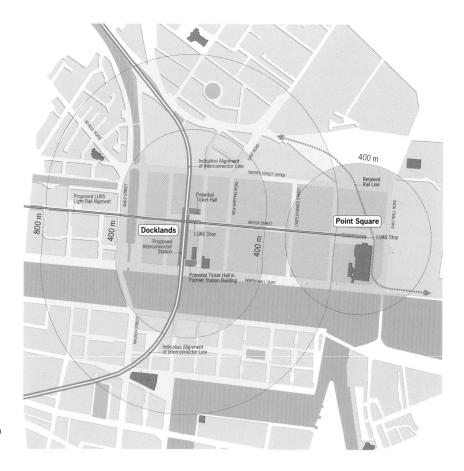

Plan showing the infrastructure of an area of Dublin.

Potential development partners and other sources of grants might include:

- Regional development agency
- English Partnerships
- European Regional Development Fund (ERDF)
- Housing Corporation
- Housing associations
- English Heritage
- Arts councils
- Heritage, Arts, Sports and New Opportunities Lottery Funds
- Sports Council.

Competing developments

What other developments or potential developments are likely to compete with development here?

Infrastructure requirements

How are infrastructure requirements likely to influence the feasibility of development?

Such requirements might include:

- highways
- drainage, including sustainable urban drainage systems (SUDS)
- services.

Costs of building and of providing related infrastructure

Affordable housing
What need for affordable housing has been identified?

Community facilities
What community facilities might be required?

Planning obligations
What planning obligations might be appropriate? (See pxx)

Incentives
What incentives might be provided to encourage good planning and design (in relation to additional floor space, council sites and planning obligations, for example)?

LIVERPOOL JOHN MOORES UNIVERSITY
Aldham Robarts L.R.C.
TEL. 051 231 3701/3634

Planning and design principles

What planning and design principles should be followed in developing the area or site?

Urban design guidance is a way of explaining how, in view of the local context, the form of development can achieve urban design objectives. The purpose of guidance is to set out principles on matters of importance, and often the process that should be followed, but not to prescribe in detail how development should be designed. The level of detail in which the planning and design principles are described and illustrated will depend on the type of guidance, on the circumstances and on who prepared it.

Sustainability

Planning and design principles should always be drawn up so as to promote development that is sustainable. Sustainability is the degree to which development is likely to have a positive impact on the social, economic and environmental conditions of people at other times and in other places.

Performance criteria

The clearest and most helpful way to express guidance's principles is often by setting out performance criteria. A performance criterion is a means of assessing the extent to which a development achieves a particular functional requirement (such as maintaining privacy). This compares with a standard, which specifies more precisely how a development is to be designed (by setting out minimum distances between buildings, for example).

The art of urban design lies in balancing principles that may conflict with one another. Standards demand to be met, and in some cases may be too inflexible to be of use in achieving a balance. Performance criteria, however, make no prior assumptions about the means of achieving a balance. Planning and design principles based on performance criteria can be expressed as: 'Development will be permitted provided that...'.

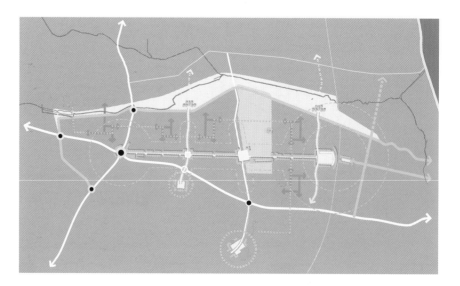

Diagram showing the basic concept for the development of an area of Dublin's northern fringe.

Design concept

What is the central idea on which the design is based?

Preferred uses

What land uses would be preferred, acceptable or unacceptable?

Mix of uses

What mix of uses is appropriate?

Proposed disposition of uses

How should future uses be arranged in the area or on the site?

Features to be retained

Which of the area's buildings or landscape features should be kept?

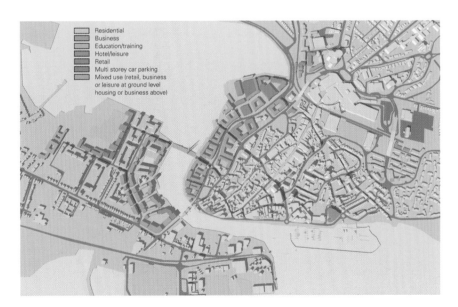

A plan of the land uses proposed for new development in Poole, Dorset.

The broad land uses proposed for a new community.

The form of new development

By Design (DTLR/CABE) identifies eight aspects of development form. These are urban structure; urban grain; landscape; density and mix; height; massing; details; and materials. (Urban structure and urban grain are aspects of layout; height and massing are aspects of scale; and details and materials are aspects of appearance). Urban design guidance should describe how development form can help achieve the seven objectives of urban design identified by *By Design* (character; continuity and enclosure; quality of the public realm; ease of movement; legibility; adaptability; and diversity).

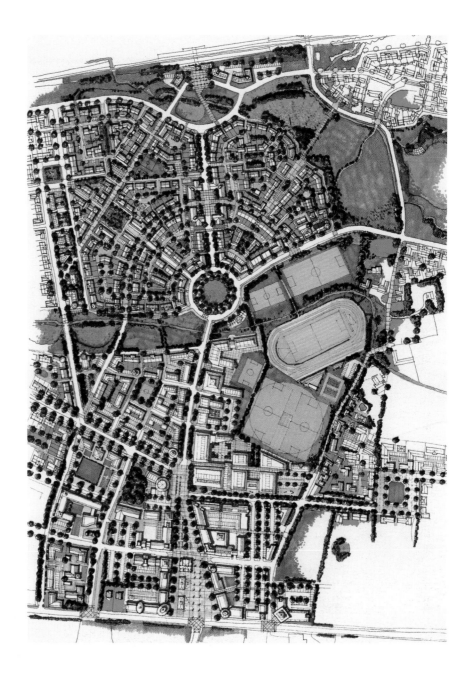

The proposed form of a mixed-use development

Layout: urban structure	How should buildings, routes and open spaces be placed in relation to each other (in two dimensions)? How should routes and spaces connect to the local area and more widely?
Layout: urban grain	How should the area's pattern of blocks and plot subdivisions be arranged? Small and frequent subdivisions create a fine grain, while large and infrequent subdivisions create a coarse grain. Where should building entrances be positioned? How should buildings (particularly their windows, active frontages and doors) relate to the public realm?

The proposed urban structure of an area of Dublin based on a new tram spine. New frontages are show in Black.

Left The proposed structure of new development shown overlaid on an aerial photograph. Below Sketches showing how the careful placing of living room windows can prevent overlooking, and how houses can provide natural surveillance of a street.

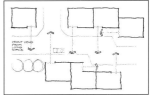

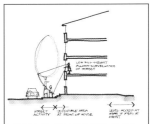

Top **Figure-ground diagram showing the fine grain of street blocks proposed for Poole.** Centre **Proposed building heights.** Below **An annotated drawing showing the sort of building forms that might be appropriate for Poole's waterfront.**

Density

What mass or floor space of a building or buildings should be provided in relation to a particular area of land?

The density of a development can be expressed in terms of:

- its plot ratio (for commercial development)
- the number of habitable rooms per hectare (for residential development)
- the area of site covered plus the number of floors or a maximum building height
- space standards
- a combination of the above.

Height sensitive zones

☆ Potential landmark buildings

1-2 storey
2-3 storey
3 storey
4-5 storey
1-6 storey
8-11 storey

Strong verticality of warehouse form of development

Use of roof terraces and set backs to building frontages add visual interest and vary sense of enclosure

Typical plot dimensions

Lively ground floor uses

6-12m

18m

6m

10-15m

8-15m wide quayside

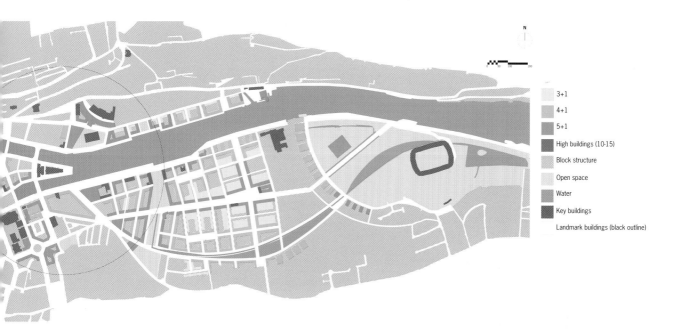

3+1

4+1

5+1

High buildings (10-15)

Block structure

Open space

Water

Key buildings

Landmark buildings (black outline)

| Height | What should be the height of buildings and structures? The following matters should be among those considered in deciding on appropriate heights: |

Diagram showing the proposed layout and building heights for an area of Cork.

Height

What should be the height of buildings and structures? The following matters should be among those considered in deciding on appropriate heights:

- the relationship between buildings and spaces
- the visual impact of the development on views, vistas and skylines.

The height of a building can be expressed in terms of:

- a maximum number of floors
- a maximum height of parapet or ridge
- a maximum overall height
- any of these maximum heights in combination with a maximum number of floors
- a ratio of building height to street or space width
- height relative to particular landmarks or background buildings
- strategic views.

Massing

How should the buildings or groups of buildings be arranged in three dimensions (shape and volume)?

Details

What principles should be followed in designing the details of buildings, structures and spaces here?

Details include:

- craftsmanship
- building techniques
- facade treatment
- lighting.

Materials

What principles should be followed in selecting the materials for buildings, structures and spaces?

Relevant aspects of materials include:

- texture
- colour
- pattern
- durability
- ease of maintenance.

Proposed planting

Structure planting	Where should new planting (including shrubs, trees and hedges) be provided to contribute to the basic form of the development?
Secondary planting	Where should other new planting be provided?
Species choice	What species will be appropriate?

Hard landscape

What hard landscape (including paving and boundaries) should be created?

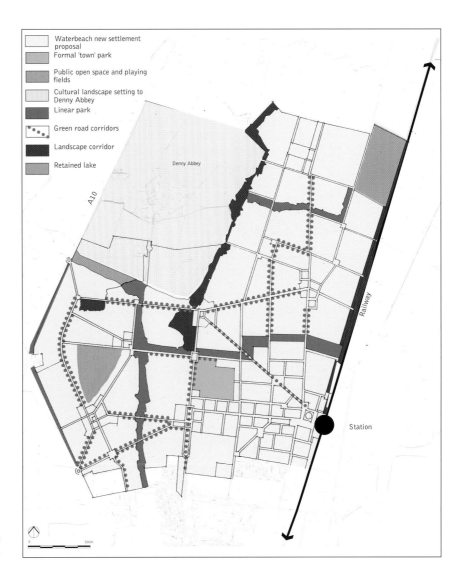

The proposed landscape structure for a new settlement in Cambridgeshire.

Open space

Public space	What public space should be provided and how should it be treated?
Enclosure	How should spaces (public and private) be enclosed?
Character	What should be the character of the open spaces?
Lighting	How should the spaces be lit?

Right Diagram showing a pedestrian movement strategy for Poole town centre. **Below left** Proposed improved access to public transport. **Below right** A public realm framework for Poole, showing the proposed network of streets, squares and boulevards.

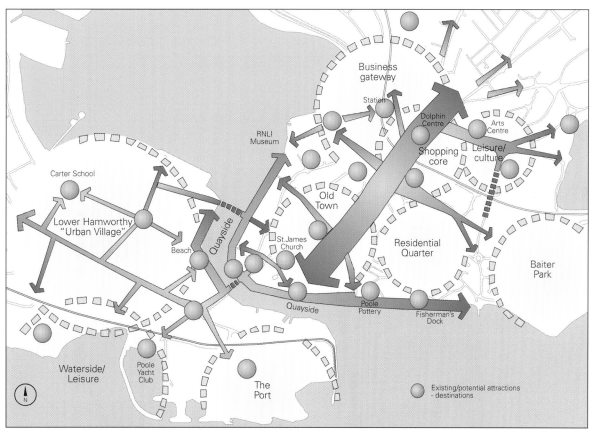

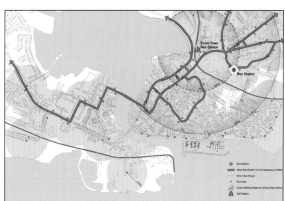

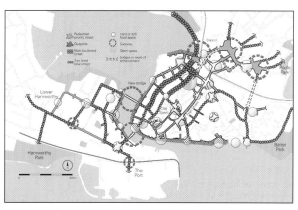

LIVERPOOL JOHN MOORES UNIVERSITY
LEARNING SERVICES

Proposed movement

Access to site	How should vehicle and pedestrian access be provided?
Access to public transport	How should access to public transport be provided?
Network of roads, footpaths and cycleways	How should a connected network of roads, footpaths and cycleways be provided?
Traffic management	What principles should apply to traffic management here?
Parking	How should parking be provided?
Accessibility for people with potentially limited mobility	How can the area or site be made fully accessible to as many people as possible?

Left Diagram of proposed pedestrian and cycle routes for mixed-use development. **Right** (above) Movement proposals for Coventry, turning part of the ring road into a boulevard. **Below** Diagram of principal routes proposed for Haringey Heartlands.

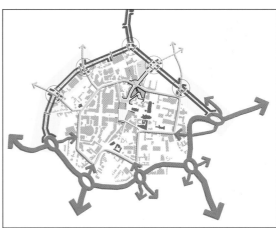

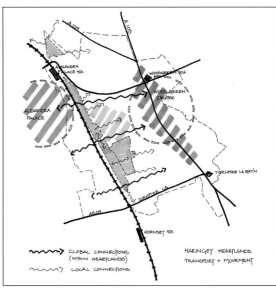

Safety

Are there any additional ways in which development should contribute to making the place safe?

Security

Are there any additional ways in which development should contribute to making property secure?

Energy use

How should development make use of solar energy (daylight, solar gain, solar panels and photovoltaic technology)?

What opportunities are there for making use of underground energy sources by means of heat pumps?

What opportunities are there for using aquifers to cool buildings?

Water

How should development reduce water run-off, minimise flood risk, and recycle water?

Wind

How should development make use of wind for ventilation or as an energy source?

Waste

How can development minimise the use of non-renewable resources (including energy, land, water and building materials)?

Public art

How should public art be used here?

Management and maintenance

How should the development be managed and maintained?

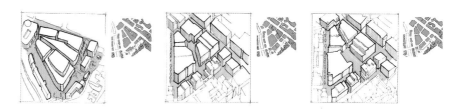

Diagrams showing alternative layouts and massing on a town centre site.

Illustrations

Concept diagrams	Diagrams showing the basic principles on which the form of new development should be based.
Building envelope guidelines	Diagrams with dimensions, showing the possible site and massing of a building.
Indicative sketches	Drawings of building forms and spaces which are intended to guide those who will later prepare the actual design.
Axonometric drawings	At 1:500 scale for a development brief.
Models	Models may be a particularly useful way of communicating to people who do not read plans easily.
Photographs, drawings and case studies	Showing and describing other examples, locally or elsewhere.

Diagram of the proposed land uses for a new settlement.

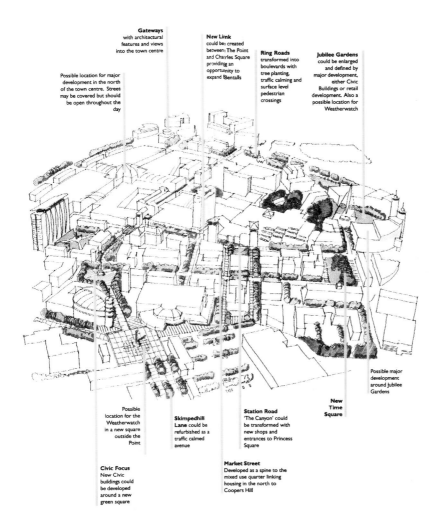

Gateways with architectural features and views into the town centre

Possible location for major development in the north of the town centre. Street may be covered but should be open throughout the day

New Link could be created between The Point and Charrles Square providing an opportunity to expand Bentalls

Ring Roads transformed into boulevards with tree planting, traffic calming and surface level pedestrian crossings

Jubilee Gardens could be enlarged and defined by major development, either Civic Buildings or retail development. Also a possible location for Weatherwatch

Possible major development around Jubilee Gardens

New Time Square

Possible location for the Weatherwatch in a new square outside the Point

Skimpedhill Lane could be refurbished as a traffic calmed avenue

Station Road 'The Canyon' could be transformed with new shops and entrances to Princess Square

Civic Focus New Civic buildings could be developed around a new green square

Market Street Developed as a spine to the mixed use quarter linking housing in the north to Coopers Hill

Above An annotated diagram illustrating one interpretation of an urban design framework for Bracknell town centre. **Below** Simple concept sketches associated with Tate Britain (left) and Waterloo Bridge and Somerset House (right) from guidance for the Thames Policy Area in Westminster.

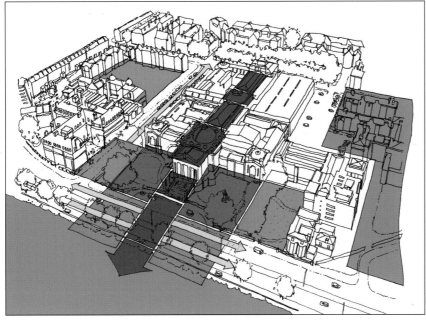

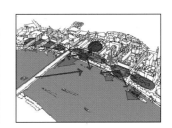

The development process

What processes should be followed in developing the area or site?

Site disposal

Method of disposal	How is the site to be sold?
Compulsory purchase	Will compulsory purchase powers be used?
Programme of disposal	When and in what phases is the site to be sold?
Programme of development	When and in what phases is the site to be developed?
Relationship between planning requirements and financial offers	How will the value of planning benefits and the potential sale price of the site be weighed against each other?
Form of submission required	Should a full or outline planning application be submitted? What form should the design statement (see p16) accompanying the planning application take? What plans should accompany the planning application? What scale should they be drawn to? What elevations, perspectives and models should accompany the planning application?

A vision of how a derelict open space in Liverpool could become an antiques market.

Design and development process

Collaboration	How will the process of collaboration be managed? Who is concerned about the future of the area or site? How should they be involved in the design and development process?
Consultation with local authority	How should consultations with and within the local authority be organised?
Consultation with local community	How should consultations with and within the local community be organised?
Consultation with other agencies	How should consultations with other agencies be organised?
Use of design professionals	What level of skills and experience will the design professionals need?
Road closures	Will road closure and diversion orders be needed?
Audits	What design audits need to be carried out? A design audit is an independent assessment of a design, carried out for a local authority (or other agency) by consultants, another local authority or some other agency or organisation.
Timescales	What is the timetable for implementing the development, including the pre-development programme (collaborations and consultations, and discussions with statutory bodies, for example).
Development phasing	In what stages should the development be phased?

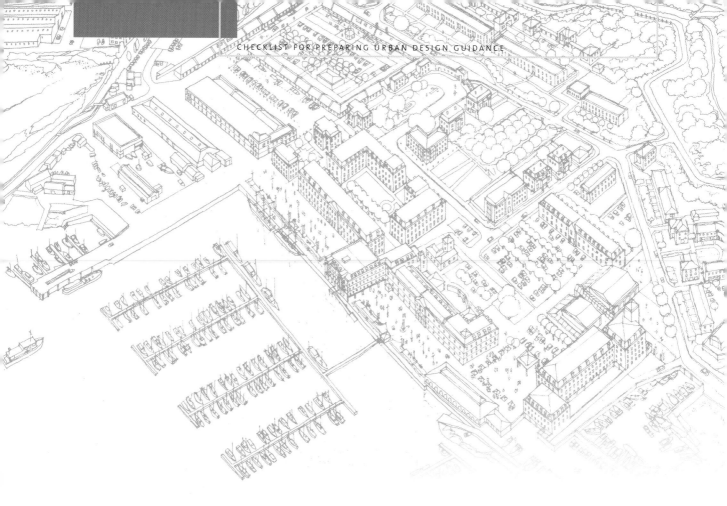

A view of how Gosport's Royal Clarence Yard and St George Barracks North might be reused.

Planning obligations

What planning obligations (Section 106 agreements) should be included in the guidance?

A Section 106 agreement is a binding legal agreement between the local authority and a developer (following negotiations between them) on the occasion of granting of planning permission. The developer agrees to provide or pay for some benefit to the locality which is required by or is a consequence of the proposed development, but which cannot be obtained by means of a condition to the planning permission. It relates to matters linked to the proposed development. The benefit is often called 'planning gain'.

Management

What management agreements or plans are needed?

Such agreements or plans might relate to:

- access
- community facilities
- landscape features
- ecological reserves
- wildlife habitats.

Further studies

Are any further studies required?

These might include:

- design impact assessments
- environmental impact assessments
- assessments of any of the topics listed above in the checklist under *Site and context appraisal* (p36).

Legal agreements

What covenants, codes and other legal agreements should be imposed?

Liability, contacts and references

Liability	To what extent is liability for the information provided in this guidance accepted or denied by the organisation issuing it?
Warranty	To what extent are warranties provided for any specialist advice given in this guidance?
Contacts	Who is the lead contact in the local authority in relation to this guidance? Who are the officers in all relevant departments and sections of the local authority who can be contacted in relation to this guidance? Who are the relevant contacts in the utilities? Who are the relevant contacts in other agencies and organisations?
References and list of other relevant documents	What documents and other sources of information should users of the guide be referred to?

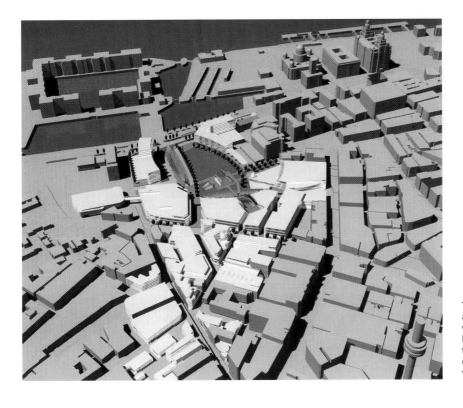

The proposed development form for an area next to Liverpool's waterfront. The urban blocks are large enough to provide the footprints for major retail use, but can be divided horizontally or vertically to allow changes of use.

Appendices

The urban design guidance should usually include:

- Extracts from the development plan.

- Extracts from other policy and guidance.

- Details of consultations
  - Statement of the consultation undertaken.
  - Summary of the representations received.
  - Statement of the local authority's response to those representations.

Proposal layout on Liverpool's waterfront.

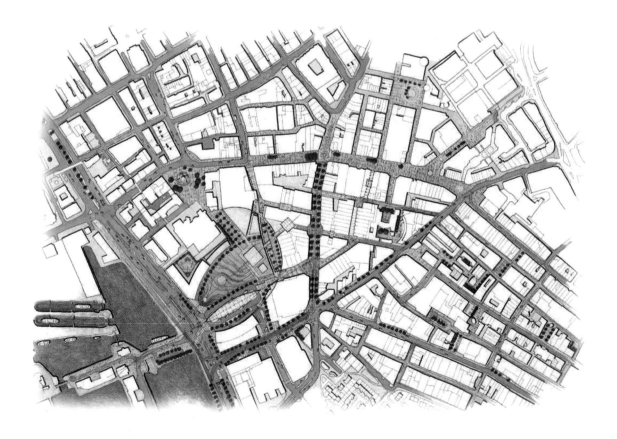

Illustration credits

Alan Baxter Associates 56 (left and lower right)

Barnsley Council 38 (top two)

Building Design Partnership 63, 64

David Lock Associates 22, 27, 35

John Thompson and Partners 60, 61, 62

Jon Rowland Urban Design 59 (top)

LDA Urban Design 32, 54, 58

Robert Cowan 10, 11, 14, 18, 19, 29 (left), 38 (bottom)

Roger Evans Associates 41, 51 (below)

Terence O'Rourke plc 28, , 49 (above), 52, 55

Tony Meats (Office of Urban Design) 29 (centre and right, and below), 36 (above)

Town Centres Ltd 39

Urban Initiatives 33, 36 (below right), 37, 46, 48, 51 (top right), 53, 56 (top right)

W.S. Atkins 43, 44, 59 (below)

Making places work

Urban design is the art of making places work. We need it in every place where buildings turn their backs on their surroundings, where segregated single-use enclaves make passers-by feel like intruders, where car parks dominate the urban landscape, where over-engineered roads put pedestrians last, and where urban and rural sites are wasted by suburban sprawl.

In 25 years of campaigning the Urban Design Group (UDG) has played a large part in putting urban design on the political and professional agendas. We must build on that achievement.

The Urban Design Group is campaigning to:

- promote best practice in urban design
- build an effective framework of policy in local and central government
- improve skills among those who shape the built environment
- show decision-makers the value of urban design
- promote collaboration in the urban design process
- make urban design and planning processes accessible to everyone

A network for change

Founded in 1978, the Urban Design Group is a campaigning membership organisation. It believes that urban design is not the job of any single profession. Making successful places depends on breaking down professional barriers, on building collaborations between the people with the power to make things happen, and on making sure that professionals, developers, councillors and communities have the necessary skills and understanding.

Urban Design Alliance

The UDG plays a central role in the Urban Design Alliance. UDAL, representing professional bodies and campaigning organisations with tens of thousands of members, carries considerable weight in working with government.

Benefits of Urban Design Group membership

- *Urban Design Quarterly*, the leading journal in its field
- *UDG News*, our email newsletter
- *UDG Sourcebook*, the guide to urban design practices, courses and sources of information
- Events, seminars, conferences and overseas study tours at reduced rates
- Regional events and activities
- For Practice members, entries in *UDQ Practice Index* and *UDG Sourcebook*, and listing on the website (www.udg.org.uk)
- Discounts on publications, training and recruitment services
- Direct mailings of urban design job opportunities (optional)

www.udg.org.uk

Urban Design Group — Membership Application Form

Name

Address

Postcode

Telephone   Fax

Email

Your employer

Name

Address

Postcode

(Correspondence and *Urban Design Quarterly* will be sent to your home address unless you request otherwise).

Course/Year (students only)

Current membership of professional institutes

Paying your subscription by standing order is a great help to the UDG.

Details for standing order mandate (to be sent to UDG)

To (name of bank)   Bank sort code

Bank address

Bank postcode

Please pay NatWest, 68 Church Street, Lancaster LA1 1LN (sort code 01 54 90) for the credit of the **Urban Design Group** (account number 89621271)

The sum of £   Amount in words

Account name

Account number

Commencing   and then every 12 months

Or send a cheque payable to the **Urban Design Group**

Please sign and return your completed application to:

Urban Design Group, 70 Cowcross Street, London EC1M 6DG

Tel: 020 7250 0892   Fax: 020 7250 0872   admin@udg.org.uk   www.udg.org.uk

Signed   Date

Gift Aid Declaration

As a registered charity, the UDG can reclaim tax on your annual subscription through the Gift Aid scheme – as long as you are a taxpayer and pay an amount of income tax or capital gains tax at least equal to the tax we reclaim (currently 28p for each £1 you give).

Please sign the declaration below if you are a taxpayer. It will not cost you anything, but the UDG will receive from the Inland Revenue tax you have already paid.

◯ *I wish the Urban Design Group to treat as Gift Aid all membership subscriptions I have paid on or after the date of this declaration.*

Signed   Date

You can cancel this declaration at any time by contacting the Urban Design Group.

Please indicate the region to which you wish to be affiliated
(Tick one only):

◯ East Midlands
◯ West Midlands
◯ East Anglia
◯ North
◯ North East
◯ North West
◯ South West
◯ South
◯ Yorkshire
◯ London
◯ Scotland
◯ Wales
◯ Northern Ireland
◯ Outside UK

Please tick membership category

◯ **Individual**	£35	
◯ **Student/Concession**	£20	
◯ **Library**	£40	
◯ **Local authority**	£100	
(includes two copies of *UDQ*)		
◯ **Practice**	£200	
(includes entries in *UDQ Practice Index* and *Sourcebook*, and listing on website)		

◯ Tick here if you do NOT want to receive mailings of job adverts.

Sponsors' details

Building Design Partnership

Location	16 Gresse Street London W1A 4WD
Tel	+44 [0]20 7462 8000
Fax	+44 [0]20 7462 6342
Email	aj-tindsley@bdp.co.uk
Website	www.bdp.co.uk
Contact	Andrew Tindsley

Roger Evans Associates

Location	59-63 High street Kidlington, Oxford OX5 2DN
Tel	+44[0]1865 377030
Fax	+44[0]1865 377050
Email	urbandesign@rogerevans.com.
Website	www.rogerevans.com
Contact	Roger Evans

Sheppard Robson

Location	77 Parkway, Camden Town London NW1 7PU
Tel	+44[0]20 7504 1842
Fax	+44[0]20 7504 1701
Email	peter.verity@sheppardrobson.com
Website	www.sheppardrobson.com
Contact	Peter Verity

WS Atkins

Location	Woodcote Grove, Ashley Road Epsom, Surrey KT18 5BW
Tel	+44[0]1372 726140
Fax	+44[0]1372 74000
Email	Richard.alvey@atkinsglobal.com
Website	www.wsatkins.com
Contact	Richard Alvey

Terence O'Rourke plc

Location	Everdene House, Wessex Fields Deansleigh Road, Bournemouth BH7 7DU
Tel	+44[0]1202 421142
Fax	+44[0]1202 430055
Email	maildesk@torplc.com
Website	www.torplc.com
Contact	Andy Ward

David Lock Associates

Location	50 North Thirteen Street Central Milton Keynes MK9 3BP
Tel	+44[0]01908 666276
Fax	+44[0]01908 605747
Email	mail@davidlock.com
Website	www.davidlock.com
Contact	David Lock

Urban Design Group

Location	70 Cowcross Street London EC1M 6DG
Tel	+44 [0]20 7250 0892
Fax	+44 [0]20 7250 0872
Email	admin@udg.org.uk
Website	www.udg.org.uk
Contact	Grace Wheatley

LIVERPOOL JOHN MOORES UNIVERSITY
Aldham Roberts L.R.C.
TEL. 051 231 3701/3634